NATIONAL GEOGRAPHIC

Ladders

TRANSFORMERS

THE QUILTERS OF

Think about all the things that you throw away. Can objects or materials be used again? In other words, can they be **"repurposed"**? By creatively thinking of new uses for old things, we can save money. For instance, consider how you would reuse old clothing.

Gee's Bend is a small town in Alabama. And several generations of women who live there have been using old clothes and cloth scraps to make quilts. These quilts are beautiful. They have bold colors and patterns. They also provide warmth in colder seasons.

GEE'S BEND

by Brigetta Christensen

What makes the quilters of Gee's Bend special? People who visited Gee's Bend saw the **artistry** in the quilters' work. The **transformation** of old scraps of cloth to beautiful art in the form of useful quilts makes the quilts unique.

NECESSITY DRIVES INVENTION

The tradition of quilting in Gee's Bend, Alabama, began at the turn of the 20th century. Many people in Gee's Bend lived simply. Their homes didn't have heating systems like homes in the northern United States. Gee's Bend is in the south, but temperatures still become chilly. People put newspapers on their walls to keep cold air from getting inside. Men and women worked long hours on their farms. And they wore through their work clothes quickly.

Families did not have the money to buy blankets to keep warm. Good material was never thrown away. So quilters used scraps of cloth from work clothes to make warm quilts.

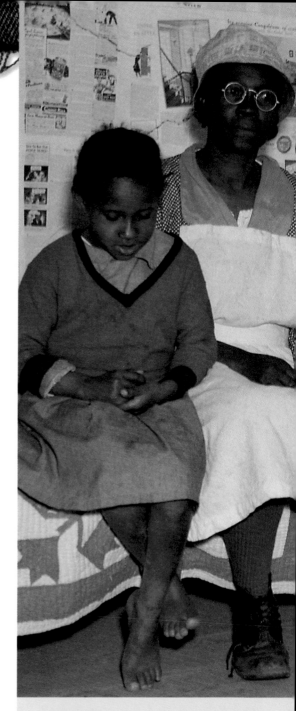

THE CRAFT OF

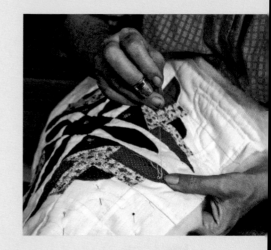

The collage effect of the newspaper wall covering inspired certain quilt patterns.

A pincushion secures pins and loose bits of thread.

QUILTING

True quilts have three layers. They have a top layer of pieces. They have a middle layer of batting. And the back layer is called backing. Putting all three layers together is called basting. Quilters may use a form to hold the layers in place as the quilt is basted. Or they may baste the layers together without the form.

Today, the stitching is usually done on a sewing machine. In the past, many quilters sewed by hand.

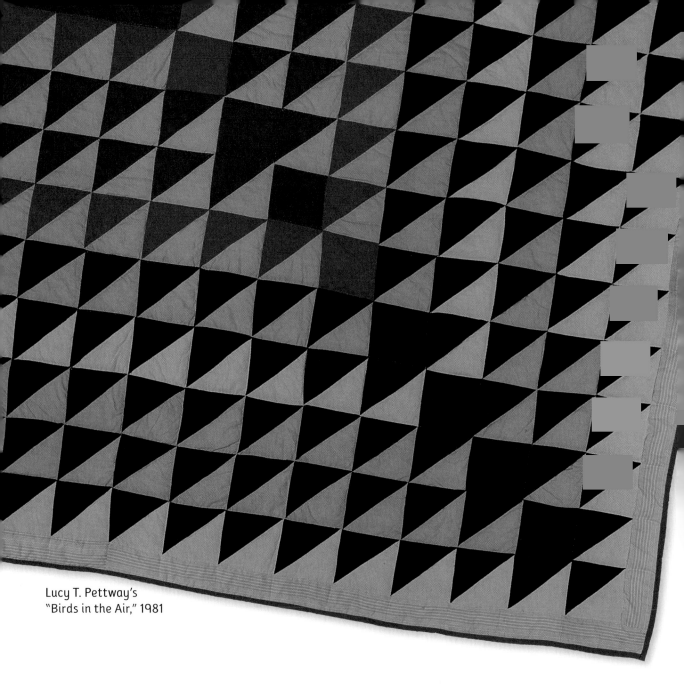

Lucy T. Pettway's
"Birds in the Air," 1981

TRANSFORMING TRADITION

In 1966, quilters in Gee's Bend formed a quilting collective, or group, called the Freedom Quilting Bee. Their work helped earn money for basics their families needed. It also provided a place to practice their craft.

The quilt collective was a transformation. Quilters used to work alone. Now they worked as a group. The technique of quilting also had a transformation. Young quilters were inspired to design their own patterns rather than follow the patterns of others.

corduroy and cotton quilt by
China Pettway, circa 1975

Arcola Pettway's "Lazy Gal," 1976

cotton quilt by Jessie T. Pettway, 1950s

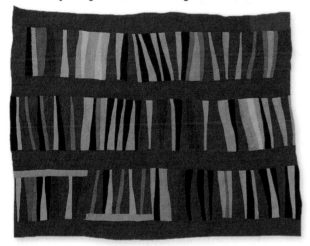

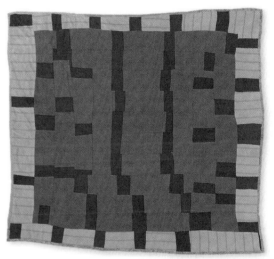

Missouri Pettway's
"Path through the Woods," 1971

Most quilters learned how to quilt from their mothers. Gee's Bend has at least six generations of quilters. They follow the traditions created by the earliest members of the Gee's Bend community. Members of the Pettway family made many of the quilts in the Quilts of Gee's Bend™ collection. Each relative used what she learned from older family members to create her own designs.

The quilters of Gee's Bend made quilts for practical reasons. Yet they followed a creative process similar to that of other artists. Their creative work and the usefulness of the quilts were both important. However, the quilters of Gee's Bend didn't initially consider how their quilts were like museum artwork. But art critics did.

Art critics saw the same quality of artistry and creativity in the Gee's Bend quilts as in the work of mid-20th century artists. The quilts have many similarities to modern art paintings.

The art world had discovered the amazing quilts of Gee's Bend. After that, the quilts became examples of mid-20th century art. Some quilt patterns have been compared to the artwork of Mark Rothko and Paul Klee. In 2002, the Museum of Fine Arts in Houston had the first exhibit of 70 quilts from Gee's Bend. And in 2003, the quilters of Gee's Bend formed a new group, The Gee's Bend Quilters Collective. The Collective is owned and run by the quilters who continue to make quilts.

No. 5/No. 22. 1950 (dated on reverse 1949). Oil on canvas, 9' 9" x 8' 11 1/8" (297 x 272 cm). Gift of the artist.

A museum curator walks through the Gee's Bend quilt exhibit. This photo shows the exhibit at the High Museum of Art in Atlanta in 2006.

These works by Mark Rothko (left) and Paul Klee (right) show bold colors. Both artists were very important in modern art movements such as abstract expressionism.

Mountain Village (Autumnal) 1934, (no 209). Oil on primed canvas on wooden panel, 2' 4 1/8" x 1' 9 1/2" (71.5 x 54.4 cm).

Nettie Young's
"Milky Way," 1971

ᴵ ᴅOING IT YOURSELF

The women of Gee's Bend passed down the tradition of quilt making out of a need to repurpose the materials they had. Many mothers told their daughters that they'd have to make all the things they wanted, like dresses, quilts, and things for their home. By making these things by hand, they learned to express themselves.

Throughout history, people have made objects by hand when they were unable to buy new items. It's fun to see what can result from simple materials and a little time and patience.

People today are returning to the crafting traditions. They are making items by hand. Some do it out of **necessity**. Others enjoy creating. This trend is called DIY (Do-It-Yourself). Some DIYers learn from family and friends. Others rely on articles or videos on the Internet. For years, people bought products without understanding how they were made. Now people are learning how to do-it-themselves. The women of Gee's Bend show that it's possible to create something beautiful from simple materials.

Check In How did the quilters transform fabric scraps?

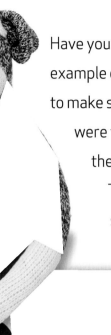

Have you ever held a soft sock monkey toy? This is an example of how people can **transform** old materials to make something new. Sturdy socks with red heels were first made for workers in the late 1890s. Using the socks, someone made the first toy monkey. The tradition continues today. Follow these steps to cut, sew, and stuff a sock monkey.

Step ❶

Turn one sock inside out. Flatten the sock with the heel centered. You will make two lines of stitches that are about $\frac{1}{2}$ inch apart, as shown in the photo. When you finish each stitch at the sock band, make a knot.

Step ❷

Make a cut down the middle of the sock between the two lines of stitching. Leave an opening near the center of the heel.

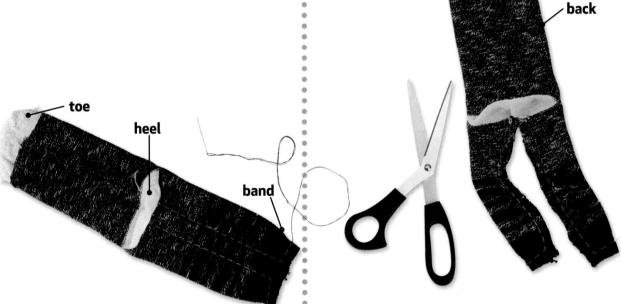

toe

heel

band

back

Materials

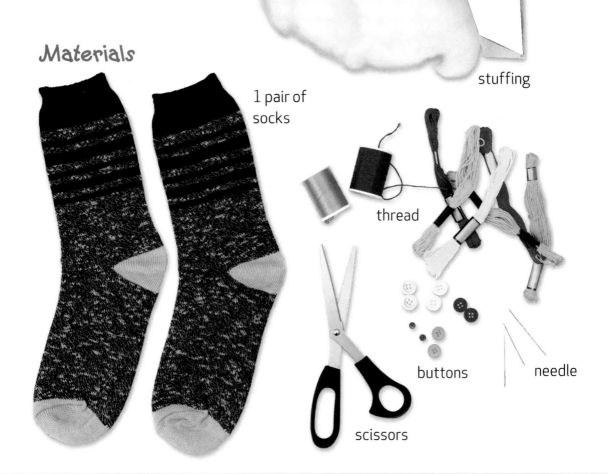

1 pair of socks

stuffing

thread

scissors

buttons

needle

Step ③

Turn the sock right side out so the stitches are inside. Stuff the sock through the opening. You will stuff the monkey's legs and upper body.

back

Step ④

Once the whole body is stuffed, sew the opening near the heel closed. You now have the monkey's body, including its head, without its mouth or ears.

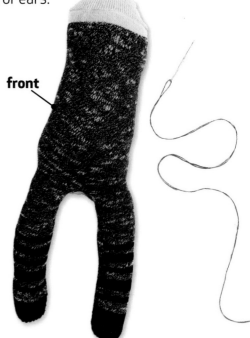

front

Step 5

Turn the second sock inside out. Cut the sock apart just above the heel. Make cuts to the bottom portion of the sock for the ears, mouth and tail. You will have one small, unused part of material.

Next take the portion for the arms and stitch two straight seams about $\frac{1}{2}$ inch apart. These stitches are like the ones you made in Step 1.

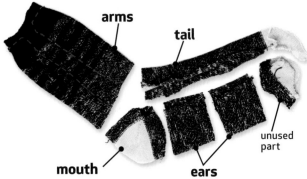

arms

tail

mouth

ears

unused part

Step 6

Set the heel (mouth) aside for now. Sew a seam for the tail and stuff it. Stuff the arms. Sew around the edges of the material for each ear, leaving a small opening in order to turn ears right-side out.

Attach the ears to the top of the toy. Close up any openings as you sew. Attach the arms and tail. Sew the body parts right to the body using small, tight stitches.

Begin to attach the mouth to the face with small, tight stitches. Leave a small opening at one corner and stuff completely. Close the opening with a final stitch.

Finish your monkey with button eyes. If the toy is for a baby or toddler, sew soft eyes using thread and stitches. Maybe even add a stitch for a belly button!

Be proud of your **handiwork.** Keep practicing these steps with other pairs of **repurposed** socks to make a whole family of monkeys!

Check In What are the materials needed to make this toy?

Urban Transformations

by Joseph Kowalski

Big cities mean a lot of people and a lot of buildings. Buildings and other structures take up open spaces. These structures and the areas around them are usually busy with activity. But for various reasons, some structures may become **abandoned.** They sit empty and unused until someone can imagine a possible **transformation.** This transformation might include ways to reuse, reinvent, restore, or **revitalize** abandoned structures and their surroundings.

From Highway to Urban Oasis

Seoul, South Korea, is a city with a population of more than ten million. A restored habitat and river run through the heart of this city. This area once had a highway above it. An urban renewal project made a transformation. The project redeveloped the old highway area into an urban park. Now there is ground level access to the Cheonggyecheon (Chung-gye-chun) River. This allows people to enjoy a repurposed part of their city. Animals and native plants have also returned to this restored habitat.

Partial structures of
the old highway in
Seoul stand in the river.

Before construction was completed, concrete structures blocked views of cityscapes in Seoul.

An aerial view during construction

Pedestrians can now walk across the river.

How did the transformation take place? It began in 2002 and was completed in just two years and five months. Construction crews first needed to take apart the old highway. Then all of the remaining structures, which blocked the stream, needed to be torn down. The project created a lot of waste. But nearly all of these waste materials were reused. Once the stream was flowing, the planners needed to think about the possibility of flooding. So the crews built embankments to withstand heavy rains and floods.

Planners also thought about the way the river looks. Plantings give the feeling of being far away from the city. Some places along the stream are great places for people to relax. The 5.84 kilometer (3.6 mile) river walk includes a waterfall, lights, and artwork. Planners wanted people to be able to easily reach the walkway. They included 17 access points from city streets above the stream. The Cheonggyecheon restoration project improved the environment and recreation options for its people. And it reclaimed a natural resource of Seoul, its water. About 90,000 people visit the banks of this urban stream on an average day.

Seoul's urban river walk is edged with concrete. Yet it offers a natural habitat that citizens enjoy.

Above New York City streets sits the High Line, a track on which freight trains used to run. The rail line was in use from the 1930s until the 1980s. Then it sat abandoned. Many wondered if the city would ever tear down the unused structure.

Two men who lived in the neighborhood had an idea to transform this old landscape. The project would turn this ugly structure into a beautiful place. The men helped create a new above-ground park that stretches across miles of city neighborhoods.

This plan for transformation would save local history and find a new use for the structure. The streets are crowded, so it makes sense to have a park above them.

New York City is short on space, so reusing existing structures, like abandoned rail lines, is smart. Also it offers a beautiful passage through part of the city.

An aerial view shows the abandoned rail line before reconstruction.

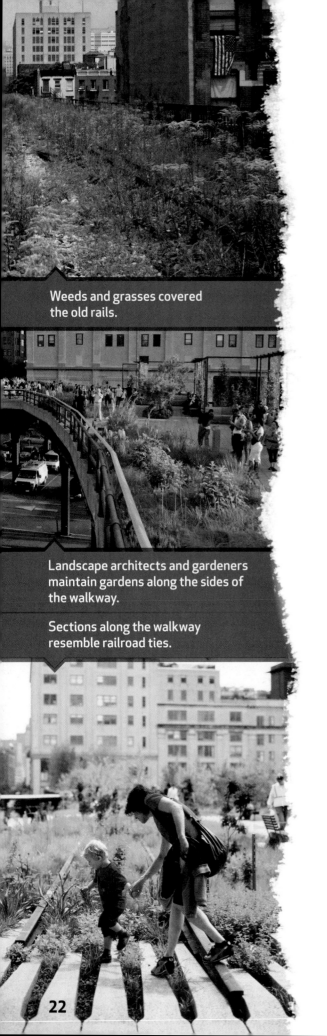

Weeds and grasses covered the old rails.

Landscape architects and gardeners maintain gardens along the sides of the walkway.

Sections along the walkway resemble railroad ties.

How was it done? The High Line had been abandoned for 20 years. It was overgrown with wildflowers and weeds. The wild growth brought some inspiration. The Promenade Plantée in Paris, France was also an inspiration. It was created from abandoned rail lines, too.

Designers competed to earn the job of park planners. The winning team built the park to reflect the original character of the track. Features like the old railway ties were left in place.

The project began in 2006 and is being completed in phases. Its development will continue. The High Line has quickly become one of New York's biggest new tourist attractions. The city and the designers combined nature with design to create a beautiful space.

In cities around the world, abandoned structures can become a revitalized space. These spaces are places to enjoy the outdoors and recall local history.

Check In What remained the same and what changed in Seoul and New York City?

23

Discuss Information

1. What connections can you make among the three pieces in *Transformers*? How are the pieces related?

2. What does it mean to be a transformer? Use information from each selection to answer this question.

3. "The Quilters of Gee's Bend" and "Urban Transformations" tell about different types of problems and solutions related to transforming old into new. What are some of the problems and solutions?

4. What would you still like to know about the people or projects in Gee's Bend, Seoul, or New York City?